Anatomy Of A Turnaround:
Changing Water Into Wine

Other Books By James R Guenther,
"The Recovering Accountant"

Management C.R.A.P. I Learned, That Seems To Work
Second Edition

Management CRAP I Learned, That Seems To Work.
Second Edition
Ebook

Anatomy of A Turnaround: Changing Water Into Wine

By
James R Guenther
"The Recovering Accountant"

Published By James R Guenther
2015

First Printing: 2015

ISBN 978-1-329-45872-7

Published By James R Guenther
17767 W Radam Drive
New Berlin, WI 53146

Table Of Contents

Acknowledgements

Thanks to my dear wife and best friend Bonnie for all her advice and encouragement and my three great kids, Jeremy, Aaron and Jami.

Then there are the grandkids, Ryan and Allison Graber who "Bupps" loves very much

Thanks to Kathy Gardner (my patient editor), and Al Haas (front and back cover) for your invaluable help in putting this book together.

Finally, thanks to my Dad, who suggested accounting as a major in college. I wanted to run a company and I did. The accounting background was a great help. Miss you Dad.

Introduction

What is a turnaround? A company is in financial trouble and has been for a while. The company is losing money. The bank that holds the loan is getting tired. After all, the bank has to justify to banking regulators why the bank is keeping the loan when there is no progress toward getting the company on track, and profitable, thereby, improving the company's ability to repay the loan and reduce risk for the bank. Finally, the bank puts the company on notice that the company must find another lender. Generally, the bank is well aware that the company will have a hard time finding new financing without a "turnaround plan". It is usually difficult and painful for company owners to do this without some assistance. Often, it is necessary to find a consultant who specializes in turning companies around. It is interesting to note that you typically can't find turnaround guys in the Yellow Pages. Most company owners wouldn't want anyone to know that they have retained a turnaround consultant. That would indicate that their company is not doing well. So, even the business cards of turnaround guys say nothing about turnarounds. They usually just state the name and phone number of the consultant.

The turnaround plan itself is a written document indicating how the company can be returned to profitability, and in a timely manner. It is presented to new, potential lenders, and obviously it is best that the plan is at or near implementation.

I never meant to become involved in turning around companies. I had spent three years in public accounting and six months in the National Guard. I then took a job as a general accountant with a very large, heavy manufacturing company. The turnaround stuff happened because in the 1970's and 1980's, manufacturing companies were going through hard times, virtually struggling for survival. My company went through expense reduction after expense reduction and I learned a lot about cutting costs. Ultimately, our company was sold three times in thirty-seven months and with the third sale, I didn't make the cut and lost my job as Controller for North American Operations. I was unemployed for three weeks and ended up at a company right next door as Vice President of Finance and Secretary for a steel foundry that seemed to be doing well, but that didn't last long. That foundry also went through a turnaround where I learned a great deal about bank refinancing and again, expense reduction. I had been at the company for about three years and I was catching on. I discovered some major flaws in the application of manufacturing burden, which was used in the sales pricing formula. I was absolutely certain that I was right about the incorrect application of manufacturing burden. Logically, why would this small foundry, with furnaces and equipment from the 1940's, have the best price in the world on small castings? Large companies shopped the world for steel castings, and they were the foundry's best customers. I took my concerns to the owner, who really didn't want to hear that the only work the company was getting was because it was significantly underpriced. I decided that if the owner wouldn't listen to me, it was time to move to another company. When I left, I told the foundry owner that they would fill up the company with small work and they would still lose money. Then, he would see I was right. My next company was a maintenance chemical company, going through a turnaround, and I was literally hired by the turnaround consultant. This would be my third turnaround from inside a company. It would also turn out to be my most rewarding and successful turnaround.

PART I   The Problems

Chapter 1   Making A Change

The telephone rang, but no one was home, so the call went to the answering machine. My younger son who was fourteen at the time, loved to regularly change the greeting on our machine and sometimes we were a little surprised at what we heard. The message the caller heard was "Hello, you have reached heaven, and this God. I can't come to phone right now because I am off judging who has been naughty and who has been nice, so please leave a message. And if you don't leave a message, well you can just go to...........beeeeep". The caller was the turnaround consultant who was working for a medium-sized chemical manufacturer and distributor. The company was searching for a controller who would serve as the chief financial officer. The consultant later told me the telephone greeting made him curious, and he just had to meet this applicant (me). So, I may in some ways owe the interview to my younger son's "cleverness". I had applied for a number of positions over the past weeks as it became clear to me that my future with the steel foundry had big limitations, since the owner wasn't going to listen to me. To make a long story short -- I turned out to be right about the incorrect pricing, and the foundry went bankrupt a few years after I left.

I later spent an hour or so, on the telephone with the turnaround guy and then met the new president of the company, who I immediately liked, and I ended up with the job of chief financial officer. I gave my notice, and left the steel foundry. I was excited about my new opportunity, but never thought this job would prove to be quite the adventure that it turned out to be.

I arrived at my new position just in time for the "downsizing" of employees. The new president and the turnaround guy had pretty much already analyzed who was going to stay and who was going to go. The company had many part-time employees and the new president had determined he wanted full time employees instead. The president and I did all the layoffs, which is never a pleasant thing to do. I just focused on the fact that some people had to go in order to preserve the jobs of the others. The layoff serves a number of purposes. First of all, it allows the company to get rid of all the "dead wood" employees, and mediocre performers. Secondly, it serves as notice to the remaining employees that management is serious about change and a new day has arrived. Generally, the remaining employees are very thankful to still have a job, and more than willing to follow the new management.

Chapter 2   The Company

The company was family-owned. The founder of the company had passed away a number of years before. Remaining were his wife, two sons, and a daughter. The founder's wife and daughter were inactive in the business but did receive a salary (which in my mind, was not proper). The younger son was the president. He had a year and a half of college. The older son was the operations manager and had just completed his third drug rehab. The turnaround guy had determined that both sons were not able to effectively run the business and in order for the bank to prevail with the company for the turnaround process, both sons were to become inactive. Their salaries would continue and they would remain as board members, as would mom. The owners were desperate to save the company and their livelihood. They were out of money and the bank had called the loan. It is my opinion that owners of companies will not implement the necessary changes to save their company until the situation is desperate and there is no other way out. Company owners so often think their companies are different, and outsiders just don't understand. I find their reasoning clouded. Companies and industries have subtle differences, but the principles upon which we run good businesses are pretty much the same everywhere. Good management, effective controls, decent markets, a quality product, attention to detail, are all necessary to run a business anywhere.

There were actually three operating legal entities: A chemical manufacturer that made products for the chemical distributor, and then another Canadian chemical distributor. The chemical manufacturer had been run pretty well and sold to many other unaffiliated distributors as well as to the two distributors that I was trying to turn around. The chemical manufacturer had about 50 employees, and the chemical distributors about 300 additional employees.

The company made chemical products used in the maintenance of almost any company or business. Everyone needed products like these. One of the salespeople used to say to new salespersons that they would pass more business on the way to their first call than they could write in a year. Surface cleaners, bowl cleaners, detergents, insect sprays, tile cleaner, bacterial products, drain cleaners -- the list goes on and on. There were approximately 1,000 products. Generally, they were a high-quality product that worked very effectively. Interestingly, they were priced about 40% lower than major competitors and there hadn't been a price increase in eight years. Why would that be? Well, obviously the owner's son listened to the sales people more than anyone else and they didn't want a price increase. Why is that? Because the easiest thing to sell is price. If I have a low price and high quality product it makes a sale much easier. Also, if you have an average cost increase of 3 % per year over eight years, that means you have lost about 24 margin points. It was now clearer as to why the company was losing money. Pricing was a major concern. The first step in any turnaround is to determine if you have a business that can make money. It appeared this company did.

Between the chemical manufacturer and chemical distributor there were two large buildings, with a total of approximately 100 employees working in both buildings.

The chemical manufacturer did a lot of what was called "private labeling". They put their products in containers with another company's label. Generally, the chemical manufacturer sold to distributors, who then sold to end users. 80% of the sales for the distributor I was working with, were to government agencies. The maintenance department in schools, highway departments, counties, states and the federal government were primary customers. That made the business fairly recession proof, because the customer revenue came from the tax base. The company actually sold Red to Green Bowl Cleaner to the White House. You introduced red bowl cleaner into the toilet bowl, and when it was done "cleaning" the water turned green. This was characteristic of many of the products. They were "gimmicky", but they worked very well.

Chapter 3   The Employees

Starting a new job was always exciting for me. My strategy had always been to "lay in the weeds" and find out what was really going on. The first step was a lengthy discussion with the president to gather his insights. Then there were meetings with my direct reports. More information gathered. My responsibilities included human resources, payroll, all accounting, purchasing, and information systems. The founder's son had been the head of the sales department, as well as president, and those duties now fell to our new president. That meant a significant amount of time on the telephone with close to 250 salespeople located around the U.S. and Canada. I very much liked the new president. He and I complemented each other. He knew the company, the employees, our markets and customers very well. I knew finance, accounting and banking very well. He was also a very logical down to earth individual, and amazingly, he and I saw the world pretty much the same way. He had purchased another company that grew bacteria and had recently left our affiliated chemical manufacturer to run his own company. He explained that he had to come back because our affiliated companies were his biggest customer. I didn't know it at the time, but he had every intention of going back to his company as soon as he could. I would become President and CEO eleven months after I started as CFO.

I had replaced the former controller, who had been let go. Her incompetence had become apparent very quickly. In addition, she had purchased a bed and breakfast a year or so earlier, and I am told she was more interested in that business. She had insisted that there were millions in cash, but couldn't pay any bills because there was no cash in the bank. The inventory was also completely screwy and the books and physical inventory had little similarity. Luckily,

I had one very good accountant who had also worked for the affiliated chemical manufacturer and our new President. The accountant was very calm, methodical, very accurate, and willing to do whatever it took to get the job done. I loved his "can do" attitude.

The chemical distributor was the largest of the companies, and sold maintenance chemical products through direct salespeople nationwide. The morale of the office employees was very poor. They had their wages reduced twice in the last six months. I was never a fan of reducing wages and salaries because every time the employee received their paycheck they were reminded that there wasn't as much money there as there had been.

The founder believed in a strong, well-paid sales force. He built the business by attracting sales employees from other companies. Maintenance chemical companies constantly competed for sales employees. Sales employees had employment contracts but there was constant legal maneuvering between competing companies. Sales employees received commission on what they sold, but paid their own expenses. They received a weekly "draw" against commissions. Accounts were settled at the end of each month, but often times the salesperson's commission didn't cover the draws, and the employee went into what was called "due company". If the sales employee quit and went to another employer, it was very difficult to collect the money due. The strategy of the founder was to make sales employees feel "special". He did this by giving different employees special benefits. His methodology was to say, "Joe, you are doing a very good job and I'm going to do something for you that I don't do for any one else. I'm going to pay for the insurance on the car you use for work". The founder was also available to sales employees almost anytime day or night. Essentially, EVERYBODY worked for the founder. There was no chain of command. That sales employee felt special. It worked. The problem was that the payroll was a nightmare because every sales employee had a different deal. The founder was a yeller and a screamer and if a sales employee complained about anything it was an office employee who drew the founder's wrath. The founder was also never wrong about anything. I observed that the only office employees who could survive were the ones who simply endured the founder's rants. Office employees shut up and did whatever the founder wanted. For me, getting information about what was going on, and what had gone on, was not easy. Understandably, office employees were not likely to tell you how they really felt about anything.

The twenty or so plant employees worked in a 35,000 square foot warehouse. The chemical distributor sold under seven different brands. The brands were the remnants of the different companies the founder had purchased over the years. The plant was in significant disarray. There was not a bin location in the whole place. Shipments of chemicals came in and were put on a shelf. You literally had twenty people wandering around with order sheets trying to locate products to fill orders. The employees were, basically, paid minimum wage and the company got its money's worth. Turnover was constant. The makeup of the products among the brands was often very similar, but salespeople were assigned to different brands and in a number of cases competed with each other. Woe onto the warehouse employee who shipped the wrong brand to a salesman's customer.

The sales employees had been considered the most important people in the company for many years. The sales force was aging or semi retired, and not a lot of new hires were staying. The retention rate for sales employees after the first year of employment was 9%. Time and money was being spent to train new hires and basically it was for nothing. Sales materials, and training, were almost non-existent. Training was done by the employee's sales manager, and of course, was as good or bad as the sales manager. Sales managers received override commissions on their salespeople. It didn't take long to figure out that a lot of managers didn't sell or work at all, but made due living off of overrides. In order to qualify for health insurance paid for by the company, and to qualify for the annual sales trip, a sales employee had to sell $50,000 in a year. Sales managers automatically qualified for the trip. That target hadn't been changed in years. Sales employees received a commission of about 30%. If they discounted off of list price, the discount was to be split 50/50 between the company and the employee under normal circumstances. But some employees could discount all they wanted, and still receive 30% of their sales. That was their deal with the founder. Sales incentives beyond commissions and the trip, virtually didn't exist. The office employee who processed commissions for payment was pretty special because she was able to remember the 250 different deals that the 250 salespeople had with the founder.

The founder could probably use a chapter all his own, but I will cover him just briefly, since he was, and is, dead. He was a strong man who had strong ideas. I surmise that he was not a big believer in education since at least three of his four children never pursued education beyond high school. One son had been killed in a plane crash some years before. The younger son had been running the company in the only way he knew how -- the same way his father did. He had about a year and a half of college and was married with a child. I found him to be an intelligent man who was way over his head and knew little about running a modern sales organization, much less a company. It was my understanding from other employees that his dad was very abusive toward him and it had been his job to carry his dad's briefcase into and out of the office. The older son was planning to move to Florida and was in that mode when I arrived. The only daughter was not married, had dropped out of high school, and had, as I understand it, four children by three different fathers. She didn't work and I'm not sure what she did.

The founder had a reputation for chastising any employee in front of anyone. As a result, he was surrounded by "yes" people. Employees kept their heads down and didn't say anything that contradicted the founder. The sales employees were always right and office employees were always wrong. The founder had his own set of rules, and was known to say, "That law doesn't apply to us", whenever an employee brought up an illegality. To me, that was just asking for trouble.

The founder had been vice president sales for another chemical company. That company had been very successful and grew at a tremendous rate. The problem was that there was a fair amount of corruption, and at least two of the officers later went to prison. The founder didn't go to prison but he did have his pardon from the Governor, for bribing a public official, hanging in the reception area right next to his membership certificate in the Kentucky Colonels. I took them down. I believe the founder started this business with the best of intentions. It was to be a company run for the mutual benefit of the sales employees. I think he meant well.

There were two people in the human resources department who were very competent. They handled office payroll, employee insurance, and served as assistants to the owners.

The purchasing manager was near retirement and seemed to have little knowledge of how a purchasing function should operate. Some of the other finance department employees seemed very good. There was an effective credit manager with three collections employees, a good accounts payable person, and a lady who did cash application. They all seemed more than willing to cooperate. I met individually with each of them.

The computer department had four employees, a manager, two computer operators and one clerical person. The jury was out on this group.

To summarize, office and warehouse employees clearly felt that they didn't matter and that no one listened to their concerns. They were poorly paid and very poorly managed. It would be necessary to improve the quality of all employees, increase wages and salaries, establish and implement personnel policies, establish standardized sales compensation, and locate managerial talent.

Chapter 4 Information Systems

Certainly, the computer changed our lives, and when I arrived at this company, we really hadn't heard much about networking of personal computers. This was the age of "mainframes", and then "mini's". Employees had "CRTs" on their desks and if you were lucky, you had a "laptop" or a "desktop" which didn't interface with the "mainframe". When I was hired, I got a laptop. That was good for me because I had a lot of spreadsheets and policies to write.

The "new" company computer had been purchased a year and a half before I arrived, when the old system had completely collapsed. The "new" hardware was 13-year old Burroughs equipment and the software (obviously to run on 13-year old equipment) couldn't do very much. During the implementation of the "new" system, the company had lost six weeks of shipping and billing. It became clear that the old management had little appreciation for computers and systems. Who knows what the "old, old" system was like? It was my understanding that the budget for the new hardware and software was $25,000. A pittance. Didn't anyone ever hear of leasing? It was my understanding that the equipment and system had been selected by the former controller and the president.

In an effort to try and salvage the investment the company had made, management had hired the consultant who implemented the "new" system. It became apparent very quickly that changes were necessary in information systems.

Chapter 5

Order Entry & Plant Operations

The warehouse was a large, concrete block building that was filled with a lot of racking. There were large tanks that were used for storage of product, mixing products and filling smaller containers. According to building codes and good safety practices, some of these tanks were supposed to be diked in case of a chemical spill -- to avoid chemicals going down the sanitary sewers. They weren't. It was expensive to dike the tanks, and besides, as the founder often said, "that law doesn't apply to us". Another issue.

The plant workers were paid from $6.25 to a high of $12.00 per hour. Turnover was very high, and the warehouse managers were almost always in a hiring mode. Just getting employees to show up for work was a constant problem. There were continual complaints from the salespeople about late shipments, incorrect shipments, or no shipments. On average, it took from seven to ten days from the time an order was placed until the product left the warehouse. Think of it -- 1,000 different products and seven different brands and not a bin location in the whole place. Because material was going in and out all of the time, where a product was this week, may not be where it was last week. Essentially there was an employee assigned to an aisle. That person was responsible for knowing what was in his or her aisle and then directing order pickers to the product. The order pickers literally wandered around trying to fill orders.

Ninety-five percent of shipments went by United Parcel Service and at this time, UPS was basically the only game in town. Just to make things interesting, UPS put us on notice that we had made two air freight shipments of paint, which was forbidden. In addition, the product had not been labeled as paint. That was also causing us problems with the Federal Aviation Administration. In order for UPS to keep taking any of our shipments, I had to write a letter of apology and guarantee that there would not be a recurrence of the error. I hated writing the letter, since UPS was, in fact, a vendor, but there was no other practical way to make shipments. FedEx was just starting to make nationwide shipments, and their independent drivers were slow to deliver to out of the way locations. So, I wrote the letter and put the UPS department on the list of things to correct.

Behind the concrete building, a huge shed had been attached. It was about 150 feet long, 50 feet wide, and at least 25 feet high. It was filled floor to ceiling with 50 gallon barrels that contained chemicals, but no one knew what was in them! As the company had closed other chemical companies it had purchased, instead of disposing of the chemicals properly at the closing of the plant, it had the inventory shipped to this plant. Here was another potential accident waiting to happen. There was a deep drainage ditch behind the shed and I could just picture chemicals running into the ditch from our shed.

Order entry is an important function in any company. If you don't get the order right in the beginning, you have a small chance of getting it right for the customer. The order entry department had about ten people trying to do an almost impossible job. Keep in mind that the company sold under different brands and in many cases, different brands had different names for the same product. In addition, products had absolutely no product codes so the order entry person had to read a salesperson's handwritten description of the customer's purchase, and the handwriting often left a lot to be desired. The order entry manager made a great effort, but she didn't have the power or support to really help her people do better work. The order entry employees were beaten down, because if anything went wrong, it was their fault. As mentioned previously, the founder consistently took the side of the salespeople, and order entry employees were right on the firing line.

Chapter 6　　　　Finance

Originally, the company was short of cash and the bank had stopped making advances and asked the company owners to pay off their loans and find another lender. By this time, the founder's sons were pretty well out of options. Maybe surprisingly, the family had no money to invest, and decided to go with the bank's recommendation for a turnaround consultant. As mentioned earlier, the turnaround guy had determined a new president was required, moved him into place and, additionally, had frozen the payables prior to my arrival. The controller had also been dismissed. The good news was that when I walked through the door, there was approximately $1,000,000 cash in the bank, and the company had been paying down debt at $25,000 per month and living on its own cash. This was a tribute to the turnaround guy, as far as I was concerned. The bad news was that payables were out more than sixty days, a lot of vendors were calling for payment, and most didn't want to extend credit.

There appeared little control over anything. Employees had no idea about approval levels or who was authorized to do what. I found that, basically, any invoice that came in got paid with no approvals or purchase orders. Inventory was a mess and every time a physical was taken, the comparisons ran differences of $20,000 to $50,000. We decided to keep taking physicals monthly, until we got it right. It was amazing that plant employees informed us that certain items on the shelf were not to be inventoried, but they didn't know why. With high turnover of employees in the plant and no bin locations, it wasn't surprising that inventory tabulation was inconsistent.

The books listed three yachts.　The employees knew where one was, and they were insistent the other two existed somewhere.

The purchasing manager just made telephone calls to order items, and never filled out a purchase order, although the form did exist. Purchases were made by almost anyone, and the purchasing manager had little clue as to what was being purchased by others. That didn't make him very accountable.

In a number of cases, wives of employees were being paid commissions earned by their husbands. The idea was to pay the wives so the employee's social security wouldn't be affected. Companies, by law, must pay only the person who earns the commission.

The balance sheet showed investments in the different companies that had been purchased over the years. The actual value of the brands, at this point, was certainly open to question. Consider this was part of the whole sales mess where certain sales employees sold under different brands and competed with each other. Also consider the mess with storing the various labeling, updating labels with legalities, not to mention order entry and warehousing numerous brands.

The company had an Employee Stock Ownership Trust, which was in violation of Securities Exchange Commission, Internal Revenue Service, and the Department of Labor Regulations, and any other agency that had anything to do with pensions and benefits. Employee statements hadn't been generated in two and one-half years, and both the administrator and trustee had resigned because of "risk" concerns.

I also found that there were numerous lawsuits relating to a lack of business licenses in a number of states, disputes over salespeople and non-compete contracts, and of course, the Equal Employment Opportunity Commission on the dismissal of a minority employee.

The subject of business licenses was a big issue. Every state requires a license to sell certain chemical products and licenses were expensive. So, the company's position had been to take out a license only after there was a sale in a particular state and then beg forgiveness. Obviously, after doing this for a number of years, the states caught on and filed claims.

The non-competes for sales people were also a constant issue. Maintenance chemical salespeople were always in demand and moved often, between competitors. Frequently, they left a "due company" at the old company which was difficult or nearly impossible to collect. So lawsuits were being filed over the "stealing" of salespeople and the company was suing former employees, trying to collect the money owed. The total "due company" on the books was well over $100,000. That "asset" was of very questionable value.

My first year-end was October 31st, and I had been there about six months. The company lost 12% on sales, but that loss did include a "house cleaning" on the balance sheet, the write-off of uncollectible "due companies", the write-off of the different brands (we had decided to sell under just two brands for two distinct markets), and, of course, adjustment to inventory. We also decided to change the year-end to December 31st and, therefore, had two year-ends in three months.

Part II   The Turnaround

Chapter 7   Changing People

One of the first steps in the turnaround process is to get the employees attention, by letting them know that things really are going to change. Employees had been hearing about changes and promised changes for years. Things were always going to get better -- soon. That first step in the attention-getting process is the layoff. Each employee had been interviewed by the turnaround consultant to determine his or her worth to the company. Many changes would be taking place, and we had a vision of a good company that paid above average compensation, had above average benefits, and was going to be a great place to work. I believed, very much, that the company could be a success, otherwise, I wouldn't have been there. I told employees that I had been through this experience twice before and I knew what had to be done. The new President and I made it clear that we would meet with any employee at any time for any reason.

We told employees we were restoring the pay cuts they had endured previously. We also announced that we would suspend the ESOT (Employee Stock Ownership Trust) and set up a 401(k) retirement plan within sixty days. If we could get these things done, the employees would start believing in us.

As previously mentioned, the controller had been fired by the time I arrived. The accountant who had been dedicated to the sister company had a good reputation within the company. He was brought over to take responsibility for the accounting of both companies. He was in place when I arrived and I found him to be extremely willing to help in any way he could. I shudder to think how difficult things would have been without him. One of the interesting things this guy did was to pile files and papers on all of the chairs in his office. It took me a while to figure out, that meant no one could sit down in his office (including me) and you were much less likely to "sit and talk".

I also mentioned the purchase of a 13-year old Burroughs computer with software that was unknown to me. I decided to replace the information systems manager. I wanted someone whose judgment I could trust. I wanted new hardware and software. I wanted IBM and I wanted to select software that would meet the majority of our needs. I had done my Master's thesis on the implementation of a new software system for a much larger company, so I had some idea of how to go about the selection process. I had also just been through the same process at the steel foundry. Almost immediately, after I had left my previous company, I had been contacted by the information systems manager. He wanted to know if I had a place for him. When I determined our existing information systems manager had to be replaced, I made the call to my old co-worker. He jumped at the chance. After he was on board, I told him he had one month to determine whether the old hardware and software could be adapted or whether we should start over. He came back to me in two weeks and said, "Start over." This was around October 1st. We discussed the hardware and software we wanted. Together, we had made a selection at our old employer, so we had a pretty good idea of what would work for us. I told my new manager that if he could implement the new hardware and software by December 1st, I would give him $10,000. That was a pretty good bonus for a guy making $40,000 a year. I am happy to say that he did it.

The existing purchasing manager, after discussions about how I wanted things changed, especially making him accountable for all purchases, decided it was just too much for him and he elected retirement. That gave me the opportunity to look for a new manager, with the kind of purchasing experience I wanted. I hired a new purchasing manager who turned out to be very well-suited for the job. He immediately began tracking the savings that he was achieving, which was averaging 10% - 20%.

There was a plant manager, an assistant plant manager, two warehouse "lead" people, and a "lead" person for the UPS department. The plant manager had been promoted to assistant purchasing manager before I arrived. He had been very unhappy about the pay cuts and was very verbal to anyone who would listen. He decided to quit the company, but then later decided he wanted to stay. We really didn't need an assistant purchasing manager. He asked me why I had allowed another employee to return after she had quit. I told him that her circumstances were different, and I wanted her back and that I didn't want him back.

There was a talented young man who was in charge of maintenance for the sister company. His brother was a very good plant manager for the sister company, as well. We figured that if we promoted the maintenance supervisor, his brother wouldn't allow him to fail. After some bumps, it turned out great. The bumps related to this new young manager who was a little arrogant and treated his people in that manner. That was not my style, for sure. I had received a visit from the lead person in the UPS department, who worked for the new manager. He tearfully (really) described the mistreatment that was going on in the warehouse, and begged me to look into it. I did, found truth, and discussed it with our new plant manager. He was very receptive to change and we had a good outcome. I was getting the organization and the control I wanted in the plant. The warehouse employees were beginning to work together.

The younger son of the founder had headed the sales department, in addition to being president of the company. His primary responsibilities had been taking calls from all of the salespeople, trying to run down the problems on orders they had placed. As part of the turnaround, the younger son had to leave the company. The reasoning was that the company was in so much financial and legal trouble that no one would believe that there would be a fresh start with members of the family still in charge. A new vice-president of sales was needed. This was a very key position in the company. Keep in mind, every salesperson had their own "deal". There was no organized incentive system. There were no written policies or procedures, no product codes, and a lot of products sold under a lot of different brands. Our new president was acting as head of sales and the more he got into it, the more difficulties he uncovered. The salespeople were used to calling the old president and the founder before him, for anything they needed. There were sales managers and four regional sales managers, but all the calls went to the old president. That made our new president's phone ring a lot! So the search for a vice-president of sales was on. We advertised nationally and located a young man who worked for a much larger competitor, but had been let go. We hired him and he turned out to be ideal for our needs. He began work on a standard package for salespeople, sales managers, and regional sales managers. A big part of those packages was a very significant incentive system. He also had lots of contacts in the industry and he began hiring quality sales people at every level.

I had pledged to get the employee ESOT in compliance, and implement a 401(k) program for employees. The 401(k) was up and running in my first sixty days. I met with the company's attorney, who was more than familiar with the problems with the ESOT. I waited two weeks for them to do something and when they didn't, I fired that law firm and hired a firm I had worked with in the past. The law firm I selected was very large, had lots of resources, and we began the process of trying to get back into compliance, so the plan could be terminated. We were in violation of numerous regulations. Our strategy was to simply throw ourselves on the mercy of the agencies involved. We had to pay some fines, but we were rolling.

After telling employees repeatedly that they had to "believe in me and us", with the progress we were making, and the changes they could see, employees began to believe that we were going to be true to our word. We standardized working hours from 8:00 a.m. to 4:30 p.m., with a half-hour for lunch. Everyone worked the same hours.

I began using the word EXCELLENCE. I loved that word. I put large banners that said "Excellence in All We Do" in the office and the warehouse. I believed that employees had to be reminded, on a consistent basis, of what we wanted to accomplish. This was going to be an excellent place to work, with excellent employees, who were paid in an excellent manner. At the same time, we started to measure everything in all departments. It was not a formal quality control program, but it was a good start. The water was starting to change to wine.

Chapter 8   Consolidating Products

As previously stated, there were over 1,000 products being sold under seven different brands, the brands were other chemical companies that the founder had purchased over the years, and the idea in buying the other companies was that it was a simple way of getting their sales employees to come and work for you. The founder had also continued to carry employees that were semi-retired. It appeared to me that he just didn't consider the cost of an employee -- especially the healthcare. The other thing the founder did was, if he had an underperforming sales person in a territory, instead of firing him or her, he would just hire another person under one of the other seven brands. The idea was that the original employee would start to work harder because of the new hire. Maybe that made sense to the salespeople involved, but, in fact, the company was competing against itself. If the products were the same (same composition, same quality), and they were, there was only one thing to compete on and that was price. So, the company, at the end of the day, loses.

The first step we took was to consolidate the brands into one brand, which was the largest selling brand, so all of our sales people would be selling the same brand. There was one exception. We had a line of agricultural products that were rather well-known, and in that the agricultural chemical market was so different from our existing customer base, we decided to keep that brand. The main product was agricultural marking foam. It was used at the end of each row of crops when fertilizer or insecticide was being applied. Because the fertilizers and insecticides were so expensive, farmers wanted to be sure they were applied only once with no overlap. We also wanted to expand our agricultural chemical product line with other complementary products.

The consolidation of brands, obviously, led to the consolidation of products. We kept one of each product as long as it was currently being sold by somebody. Products were reduced to 480. This was still a sizeable offering, but better than 1,000 products. Next, we assigned product codes to the remaining products and asked the salespeople to start using the product codes when they placed their orders. This would really speed up the order entry and order picking process. The salespeople sure didn't want to start looking for product codes, so they would simply write down what they used to write down -- the product name.

The order entry manager, consistent with past practice of losing on any position she took, had her people entering product codes on orders received from salespeople. I put a stop to that by telling salespeople that if orders didn't have product codes, they would not be processed. We had a lot of grumbling, but the salespeople began using the codes. Many of the salespeople had come from other companies and were used to using product codes. The order entry manager was really happy with us. With the consolidated products, we completely redesigned all the of product labels. We obtained new artwork, commonality of labels, and improved accuracy of the label information, a huge undertaking but well worth the effort.

We also emphasized case sales. While we would still sell just one quart or gallon of this or that, we made it very expensive to do so. You could virtually buy a case for the same price. The salespeople, of course, didn't like this either. It was harder to sell a case than it was a single bottle, but the higher price helped.

Chapter 9   Fixing Plant Operations

In keeping with the addition of product codes, it was now possible to assign bin locations in the warehouse. We used plastic pouches with Velcro, so that if we needed to change locations, it was easy to do. This was especially the case in the beginning. Also, consider how the reduction in products and brands helped our inventory processes.

The personnel in the warehouse left a lot to be desired. The turnover was very high and when you paid only minimum wage, you got what you paid for. At this time, also, drug testing was just coming into play, and we, like most companies, hadn't done any.

Very quickly, we replaced three-fourths of the warehouse staff. We raised wages a minimum of two dollars over minimum wage. It was amazing to see the improved quality of employee we had by raising the amount of money we paid. Over time, we reduced the warehouse staff from twenty-two people to thirteen, and increased efficiency. This was the coming together of reduced brands, fewer products, product codes, and the improved quality of the warehouse employees.

In keeping with total quality management, we began to measure everything, including incoming and outgoing orders and errors. We made every effort to not assign blame to an individual person, but rather to emphasize improving the process. Obviously, if we had an error prone employee, we also dealt with that. We also implemented a policy of no one leaving the warehouse until all of the orders received by 11:00 a.m. had been shipped. The first time we had a customer call to complain that our invoice was arriving before our shipment, was great news and an accomplishment to me. The new warehouse manager came to me at one point and said that he wanted a permanent employee who would clean up the work stations of the other employees. I refused the request and said employees had to clean up their own workstations and still had to be out by their quitting time. I didn't think employees would be neat about their work stations if they new someone else would be cleaning up after them.

We emptied the shed attached to the main building. It had been filled with 50-gallon drums and some totes of unknown chemicals that had been brought there when other chemical companies purchased by this company had been closed down. It took seventy-five semi-trailer loads to clear the place out.

Chapter 10   Fixing Finance

I had meetings with our lender, who as previously reported had asked us to find other financing. The purpose of the meetings was simply to keep the bank appraised of what we were doing, in hopes that they would forbear until we could return to profitability. In addition to that, I was becoming very proud of the changes we were making and the success we were having.

Next, we began implementing controls throughout the business. For instance, an invoice only got paid in two ways: 1) there was a valid purchase order, or 2) an approval from an authorized manager. In order to have an authorized signer, it was required that we create a "Book of Authorized Signers." This enabled employees at all levels to know who was authorized to do what. If an employee tried to do something for which they were not authorized, employees were instructed to bring the issue to me, and I investigated, and dealt with the unauthorized person. As mentioned previously, in the past, any invoice that came in was paid. We had paid for a lot of Yellow Pages ads that we had never subscribed to. I began reviewing every single incoming vendor invoice. If I didn't understand what the invoice was, it didn't get paid until I did. The number of things I found was surprising. The company was renting three storage sheds in various parts of town that had nothing in them. I located, and sold, the three yachts. I went through a thorough review of property insurance, selected a new agent with whom I had worked previously, and saved a bunch of money by consolidating policies. If I was contacted by an insurance agent with whom the company was currently working, I had no qualms about giving them a shot at keeping the business. I also had no qualms about making changes, since I usually felt that they had not been doing their jobs with the previous managers.

There was a maintenance employee (the only one) who had a company credit card and his charges averaged between $1,000 and $2,000 per month, with various building supply companies. The man worked for the company and for the family, and it appeared that he had it made. If you asked him where he was, he would tell you he was at the family home. If the family asked where he was, he said he was at the company. He also had a side handyman business. We eliminated his job and $1,000 to $2,000 per month in purchases just went away. We simply used outside contractors for any maintenance work that was necessary.

One day, my very smart accounts payable clerk who had been really good about following instructions, came into my office with a "statement" from ABCD Insurance Agency. She explained to me that this statement was for a salesperson's car insurance, that the founder had agreed to pay, as a special deal. I had instructed our accounts payable employee that she could only pay "invoices" and never "statements". Statements are always supported by invoices. The amount submitted by the employee was about $1,600. That seemed like a lot for six months of insurance on one car. I told her to call the insurance broker and ask for the invoices behind the statement. To make a long story short, the company had not only been paying the employee's car insurance, but also the employee's wife's car insurance, his homeowners insurance, AND a markup which was ultimately refunded to the employee by the insurance agency. Our employee had developed a nice relationship with the office manager at the insurance agency, and she essentially did whatever our employee asked her to do. I fired the sales employee and received a refund from the insurance broker for everything but the employee's car insurance, going back seven years. I think I could have easily prosecuted both our employee and the office manager of the insurance agency, but I didn't. I just wanted the ordeal to be over.

The Book of Authorized Signers covered who could request a purchase order, and every purchase began flowing through the purchasing department. Employees were willing to follow new procedures, in order to get the invoices paid for items they ordered.

Then, there were the subscriptions to Commerce Clearing House Tax Services. Updated pages came in weekly, but instead of being placed in the binders, the updates were simply piled under a counter -- in the original envelopes. There had been no filing for at least three years. They were piled three feet high and about twelve feet in length. I cancelled all the subscriptions. After all, our tax returns had been completed by our accounting firm for years. Why would you continue to subscribe to a tax service when you weren't doing the taxes? Savings were everywhere.

We standardized the sales positions with salespersons, sales managers, and regional sales managers. The standard positions had standard deals. So if a salesperson had a "special deal" it was eliminated. At the same time, however, we rolled out our new sales incentive system where salespeople could win anything from a computer to a big screen TV, to cash, to the company trip. That made the loss of the "special deals" a little easier to accept. All sales employee compensation was now based on discounted net sales, and all incentives earned were based on commissions earned. We also began running regular sales contests with a variety of winners.

As mentioned earlier, I established a 401(k) plan in sixty days. It had been promised for three years. It contained a 10-cent on the dollar company match and, of course, employee deductions were made pre-tax. The match wasn't a tremendous amount, but it was still 10% interest before any investment income. I really believe that this was a great benefit for employees and I had personal meetings with those employees who hadn't signed up. I just wanted to be sure all employees understood the plan and really, how little impact participation could have on net pay.

The new law firm I hired, helped us to resolve our ESOT problems, settle lawsuits with other chemical companies, U.S. government agencies, including the FAA and the Department of Labor, the State of Texas, and the U.S. Attorney in New Jersey.

Ultimately, we eliminated salesperson draws and began paying commissions on a weekly basis. This eliminated the problem of "due company" and constantly adjusting draws. This also addressed the problem of salespeople not working the first two weeks of each month, which then eliminated the month-end rush in the warehouse, and the warehouse having little to do the first two weeks of each month. We also took the sales employees' wives off the payroll. Checks were addressed to the persons who earned them, only.

I settled a lawsuit with the Equal Employment Opportunity Commission over an alleged discrimination lawsuit. I found the complaint to be completely unwarranted, but we had no documentation to prove our position. We began thoroughly documenting employee disciplinary actions.

I settled a lawsuit with another chemical company that had been on appeal on every level. Our company had lost every appeal. It was time for it to be over. We paid out $1,000,000.

We had been living on the cash we generated for more than six months and we had paid down our line of credit with the bank by $25,000 per month. To my surprise, our bank decided to renew our lending relationship. I had not seen or heard of this before. Usually, once a bank asked you to leave, they seldom turned back. We also became profitable on an operating basis.

I sold a travel agency we owned that wasn't making any money, to its employees. I didn't want to be in the travel business.

We experienced purchasing savings of 10% to 20% with our new purchasing manager and his improved methods.

We changed auditors and filed state tax returns for the prior two years in about twenty-five different states.

I went through a thorough review of property and product liability insurance, selected a new agent who I had worked with previously, and saved more than $30,000 by consolidating policies.

We changed health insurance agents and saved about $100,000 per year on insurance with the same benefit level.

The company had very few documented policies on anything. I started over and wrote policies on holidays, vacation, payment of commissions, tuition reimbursement, performance reviews, safety equipment, and a variety of others.

We eliminated paid sick days for all non-exempt employees by giving the equivalent of three days' pay, in the form of a raise. We, essentially, bought out employee sick pay. Sick days dropped significantly. We eliminated employee gifts for Mother's Day and Father's Day. For birthdays, employees could pick from a variety of company logoed items. We did keep "Pie Day" where office employees voted for what kind of pie they wanted from the local pie restaurant. We took the top ten pie vote-getters and brought them in for all employees to enjoy -- with ice cream, if preferred.

We cleaned out the office storage area, and disposed of old records in accordance with IRS guidelines. That took four 40-yard dumpsters.

We redesigned all internal forms with the new logo and eliminated old, outdated, four- and five-part forms.

We replaced the old, outdated telephone system, with a new one, which met our requirements and had favorable lease terms.

I implemented a planning process at all levels of the company. That hadn't been done before. It included a profit plan and a strategic planning process. We had to figure out where we were going and how we were going to get there.

Chapter 11   Fixing Sales

The life blood of this company, and most any company, is sales. The number one reason that small businesses fail is lack of sales.

Outside sales is a tough job but it has its benefits, as well. It can be lonely. Field sales people often feel detached from the rest of the company, and in my experience if sales people don't feel good about themselves or their company, they don't feel like getting up and trying to go sell something. The other significant issue is that sales can be very lucrative and provide a nice life for a family. In addition to that, there is great freedom of movement and in setting working hours.

The point is that, reorganizing the sales effort, is not as easy as some other areas of the company. It has to be done with great care and a lot of repetitive communication -- a lot of communication. If I had to do this portion of the turnaround again, I would do it differently. I would communicate more effectively. There were also two sales people that we should have fired, but did not, because of sentimentality, which came back to be a significant factor in my undoing.

I mentioned earlier that the younger son of the founder was running the sales effort, as his father did. But, times change, people change, and the way companies operate must also change. We can't just do what worked previously, forever.

We had hired a new vice-president of sales. He came from a much larger maintenance chemical company and had a very effective knowledge of sales and incentives. We told him we wanted him to reorganize the sales effort from top to bottom. We wanted a standard package that applied to all sales employees. There would be increasingly good incentives for sales managers and regional sales managers.

Fringe benefits would be in accordance with IRS regulations -- no special deals.

The existing sales program was one that I'm not sure that anyone, except the founder, really knew and understood. Sales employees earned a 30% commission on what they sold, if they sold at list price. If they sold at less than list price, the discount was to be split 50/50 between the company and the sales employee. Sales employees could become managers when they hired their first sales employee. The neat thing about being a manager, was that a you earned an override commission on whatever the new employee sold. It was about 5%. If you had two or three or four sales employees, it could be a pretty good income. In return for the override commission, the sales manager was responsible for the training of the new employee, as well as encouragement, product knowledge, and sales techniques. Obviously, this system had its benefits and detractions. A new sales employee had little chance of success if his sales manager was a poor salesperson. But at the same time, a sales manager wanted his new employee to succeed. It was also not unusual for the founder to "award" a sales employee to a manger who was in favor. Also, remember that sales employees received a weekly "draw" against commissions. The draw was set by the founder's son, and he, in theory, adjusted the draw up or down based on employee sales over the past few months. Draw accounts were to be settled at the end of each month. If commissions exceeded draws, the employee received a fifth check. If draws exceeded commissions, the employee was in "due company" and the balance carried over to the next month. The draw was a problem on many fronts. "Due company" was always difficult to adjust. Surely, the sales employees didn't want their draw adjusted downward and, of course, voiced their opinions. The system was easy to abuse, because the next "big" order was always right around the corner. The ultimate slap in the face was when the salesperson left the company and went to work for another chemical company, while in "due company". Sometimes that was many thousands of dollars. The effort required in collecting the "due company" was hardly worth the cost, and then there was the logic that if the sales employee was in "due company" he had very little money anyway. Sales employees were comfortable with a draw check coming every week. Often, it seemed they didn't become worried about whether they were in commission until the last week or two of the month. When they got worried, they got out and sold -- in the last week or two of the month. So, the first couple weeks of the month, warehouse employees had little to do and the last week of the month, they were absolutely frantic. That wasn't a desirable situation from a plant operations standpoint.

Finally, one of the only sales incentives was the annual sales trip. It was usually to Florida and lasted two or three days. If you were a manager, you automatically qualified. If you were a salesperson, you had to sell $50,000 worth of products. That goal hadn't been changed in years. It was often said the trip was earned by the spouses of salespeople. The majority of sales employees were men and it was the wives who encouraged their men to get up and go out and sell, or else.

Here are some of the changes we made. First, we determined that every incentive for salespeople had to be earned. No one, including sales managers, got a free ride. We began by changing sales incentive measurement from a product sales basis, to a commissions earned basis. This focused sales employees on the commissions they were earning. It reduced discounting, returns, and freight giveaways. It had not been uncommon for a sales employee to write an order and have it shipped to a customer who never ordered anything. The idea was to get a commission check, knowing full well the commission would be charged back at some point. Previously, if a sales person gave away freight, it wasn't considered a discount and they weren't charged for it. The new vice president of sales wrote a sales policy manual, a sales training manual, and established new sales incentives and new contests which ran on a regular basis. They usually featured a specific product or family of products. The prizes were things like computers, TV's or VCR's.

We set a minimum commission level of $35,000 per year, for what was considered "employee" status. Employee status meant the array of fringe benefits, health coverage, life insurance, 401(k), and eligibility for the trip.

We changed our policy to control sales of miscellaneous products, control of consignment inventory, and limited extended sales terms. Some of our salespeople would sell anything a customer needed. One such instance was the sale of mulch to Trump Plaza. While a customer may appreciate someone who can get you anything, it took our purchasing person a lot of time to locate and purchase these miscellaneous products. In addition, we only accepted an order if there was a significant margin for the company. We had to limit consignment inventories because they were difficult to control. The extended sales terms were often offered by salespeople because they got their commission right away, and the extended terms didn't cost them anything.

Earlier, I mentioned that when I arrived, the company hadn't had a price adjustment in eight years. I refer to price adjustment, because we didn't raise prices on everything. Some prices went up and some went down, therefore, an adjustment. We watched pricing carefully as it related to price increases we were receiving from our suppliers. Significant supplier price increases led to our price increasing. The pricing review became a constant.

We set up a sales advisory board made up of salespersons and we used them as a sounding board for any changes in sales policies and pricing. Many of the salespeople seemed more comfortable addressing their concerns to fellow salespeople, rather than their sales manager. The salespeople now had a voice in the shaping of policies that affected them.

The maintenance chemical industry seemed to, attract salespeople who could be just this side of shady. We made it clear that we were going to operate within the law, ALL of the time. We made certain that our "giveaways" were always logoed products. Customers could get a free logoed jacket or shirt or hat with an order of this or that. The customers we sold to were generally maintenance employees in government type agencies: counties, highway departments, schools, cities. The most popular giveaway that we had was a camouflage cap with "scrambled eggs" on the visor. We just couldn't keep it in stock. The giveaway recipients were generally not well-paid, and were always looking for an incentive to buy. It was common for an employee to have purchasing authority of two or three hundred dollars without a company purchase order. That was about the average size of our orders.

We introduced twenty-five new products and eliminated more than one-hundred existing products. Some of the new products were pretty cool. We had a glass cleaner that had silicone as an additive. It was to be used in shopping malls on entrance and exit doors, because the silicone prevented finger marks on glass windows. Another product was a window cleaning product that neutralized cigarette smoke odor in rental cars. Everyone is now familiar with alcohol based hand cleaner. We developed that product for use by highway departments where employees didn't have access to soap and water before their lunch break. And, finally, we started manufacturing self-defense spray under the name of a large firearms company.

We also implemented a policy where office managers and upper management would travel with a sales employee on a regular basis, but at least twice a year. This promoted understanding of what the other guy had to live with on a daily basis and promoted understanding among office and sales employees.

Over the course of a year, we turned over the entire sales order entry department employees. We reduced the headcount from twelve employees to five. We were also able to significantly increase the hourly pay rate. That happened this way: I had a suspicion that we could eliminate a person from the order entry department. When an employee quit, I knew that if I asked if the person had to be replaced, the answer would be a yes from the department manager. So, I got the whole department together and told them that this was a very confidential meeting and I requested that they keep the subject matter to themselves. I told them that "Donna" had quit, and I believed we may not have to replace her. Here was the deal -- if Donna made $10 per hour, I would split the savings of her leaving with the remaining employees, 50/50. So, each remaining employee got a raise of about a dollar per hour, over and above their normal pay increases. This did two things. It increased hourly wages in a place I wanted them increased, making it easier to keep good employees. The idea of keeping this subject confidential was entirely a scam. I knew that word would get out to other departments, and sure enough, a few weeks later, an employee quit in the UPS department and I had a visit from the lead person in that department who said he believed we didn't have to replace the person who left. Sure enough, I had employees eliminating headcount!

One of the most difficult situations I had to confront was the dismissal of a regional manager. It became clear to us that this man was working full time in a store he owned and spent very little time working for our company, and very little time with the sales employees and sales managers under his direction. We decided to dismiss him, which led to threats from him and his wife. The threats included blowing up my house with my wife and kids inside. It was necessary to tell my family about the threat and tell them not to open any packages or envelopes received in the mail. I didn't think the threat was of real concern, but one never knows. We contacted the FBI and I know that they interviewed the former employee. I don't think any more came of it.

Chapter 12   How It Ended

A sales trip was scheduled to be held in Puerto Vallarta, Mexico. I didn't know it at the time, but there was a movement underway to get rid of our vice president of sales. He wasn't real well-liked by many of the old-time sales people. I thought that was pretty understandable. He had been an agent of change and had made the changes over a reasonably short period of time. I supported what he had done.

I mentioned earlier that there were two sales employees that we should have fired when we began the turnaround process. One was the best friend of the founder, close to the family, who lived out of state and really did very little work. When the turnaround began, the new president decided not to dismiss this employee because he was afraid the employee could take too many sales employees with him if he found another job. Secondly, we had an inside sales manager who was originally the founder's driver, and in my opinion, the paid best friend of the founder's son. His loyalty was to the family, not the existing management.

Months before, I had a conversation with the founder's friend. He talked about the salary reduction he had to take as part of the turnaround process, from $250,000 per year to $150,000. He insisted he wanted that money and he was going to get it -- one way or another. I told him that I would pay him the money in the form of a retirement benefit, but there was no way I could write him a check today. I believe it was after our conversation that he began plotting the demise of me and our vice president of sales. The inside sales manager, as I understood it, did a lot of snooping. He was trying to come up with some dishonesty on my part. He looked at expense reports and checks that had been written to me, trying to find something wrong. He and the family just couldn't believe I wasn't doing something dishonest. Maybe that says something about them.

A meeting was held with the family, the two above individuals, and some of the regional sales managers in Puerto Vallarta. My information comes from a sales employee who was present at that meeting. The group wanted the founder's son back as president of the company, and the new vice president of sales out. Some folks wanted me gone, as well, but there was apparently little support for that. My contribution to the company was well-recognized. When we were all at the airport getting ready to leave Mexico, the founder's son told me he was going to run the company again and he wanted me to return to the position of chief financial officer. I told him I couldn't do that. I simply couldn't work for a person that I considered dishonest and unethical.

Three days later, I received notice of a special board meeting. I surmised it was for the dismissal of me and our vice president of sales. I left town so it would be difficult to serve me with any paperwork. That was the end of my tenure at this company. I didn't have a golden parachute, but I did have a contract that paid me full salary for a year. That gave me time to think about what I really wanted in life, which was to help people. It didn't matter what I did, as long as it involved helping people. I took a job as CEO of a non-profit focused on financial education for kids. It was a great job, where I met and worked with some of the nicest people in the world.

Perhaps I should have hated the family. After all, I spent a lot of time saving their company. I did something they couldn't do and I did it well. But I didn't hate them. I went in as a hired gun and I knew that from the beginning. At some point, it was likely some member of the family would want to run it again. After I left, I heard a lot of the talk emanating from the company. Someone said the reason for my departure was that the company was not profitable. It wasn't the day that I left, that was true. But keep in mind, the company's year-end was the calendar year-end, as well. I left in early April and I don't think the company was ever profitable in the first three months of any year. Three months just didn't generate enough sales volume to cover the fixed costs. I am certain the company was profitable for the year and, in fact, the company still exists today, so I must have done something right. Right?

Chapter 13   What I Learned

This was my third turnaround and in each of them I learned more than the last time. These experiences changed the way I looked at my work, my family, and my life. I think I became a better, more sensitive individual. My experiences sure did instill a love of people of all colors and backgrounds. From a work standpoint, I learned to make judgments very quickly on who I wanted with me and who I had to let go, hopefully, to find and better themselves with their next work experience.

One of the more important lessons that I learned was to hire and work with the right people. You must have the right people "on the bus" and "in the right seats on the bus". In addition, when you find you have a wrong person on the bus, remove them. Don't transfer, don't "retrain". Don't wait for a change. Just remove them from the bus. Make those decisions for the good of the company, not for the good of you, or the department, or the other employees. Look only at the good of the company.

Believe and listen to the good people you have retained and hired. Make them focus on improving the "process", the "system" instead of trying to lay blame on individuals. Listen closely to what your good people have to say. There are improvements that can be made every day in every department in every company. It is too bad that in so many companies, employees don't suggest improvements because the employees think their suggestions will fall on deaf ears. Encourage everyone to come forward with meaningful measurements for their job, department, and the company. Measure everything. That will help managers to become proactive rather than reactive.

Raise prices and lower costs on a consistent basis. Raising prices is hard, and don't expect to get any congratulations from your sales staff. Remember, the easiest way to sell is if you have the lowest price and the highest quality product. Often the two can't go hand in hand. It is much harder to sell high quality than it is to sell low price. We should always strive to be the low-cost leader in our industry, because that means we can make money when our competitors cannot. We have to keep the pressure on our purchasing and manufacturing departments to continue to seek out ways to lower costs. That is hard, because those folks are busy generating product. Thinking about cost improvements takes up valuable time. I have often said that thinking is hard work and that's why we don't see more of it.

Make good decisions, or maybe, don't do dumb things. I have seen so many instances where managers make poor decisions because they let other issues cloud their thinking. Those issues may be, what other employees think of the person or process, whether a person is well-liked or hated, whether the person is a long-term or short-term employee, whether the employee is a friend or relative of someone else in the company. You get the drift. Focus on what is best for the company and nothing else.

Listen. Easy to say, yet often hard to do. Each of us has our own set of biases and beliefs. So often, when managers are hiring, they subconsciously try to hire themselves, obviously because the way they look at the world is the best way, or so they think. Listening objectively takes really hard work. We must open our minds and believe in the good people that surround us. When in doubt, give it a try. You can always change back.

Practice MBWA. "Management By Wandering Around". I so believe in this concept. I have been very surprised on many occasions about what I have learned from my fellow employees that became so helpful somewhere down the road. This is another method that helps us be proactive instead of reactive in our business.

Personally, watch your balance sheet. Know in detail what is in your inventory and what is in your receivables. Pay particular attention to balances that have been stuck there for a while. Make every effort to get rid of them. I have come across many business owners and managers that really don't understand the balance sheet. It is essential to understand it!

Make customer calls on a regular basis. Encourage your senior staff to do the same. There is little that is more informative than talking to your customers. Travel with your salespeople, especially those on the ground level. They enjoy it, customers tend to be flattered, and you learn a lot.

Unfortunately, in today's litigious environment, document employee disciplinary actions and don't lose heart. It may take a while to get the right people on your bus, but keep working at it.

Finally, make planning a part of your business life. There is operational planning, profitability planning, strategic planning, and even business continuation planning. I have observed a lack of planning in so many different businesses. Owners and senior managers are worried about orders coming in the door and orders going out the door, that there just isn't time for planning. The top guy has to make time and make sure senior managers do the same.

There have been many times when I sincerely thought I was the only one in the company who did any real thinking. I have employees come through my door and describe their problem and, perhaps, ask a question. My reaction was often to ask them what they thought was the "right" answer for the company. Nine times out of ten, they came up with the right answer. They just hadn't really thought through the problem. It is sometimes necessary for us to help our employees THINK!

I came to this company as the chief financial officer and I believe I was very well-prepared for the position. I have never struggled with the accounting side of things. If you didn't know something, it wasn't very hard to find out the answer. It is true that a lot of accounting is black and white, with very little gray. People are a different story. People are always a challenge. Sometimes, what we say to person A is exactly the right thing and exactly the wrong thing for person B, in the exact same situation. As I look back on my experiences in preparation for this job, the first thing that comes to mind is the way that my father treated his employees. He was a banker and well-liked by his employees. He was compassionate, fair, honest and frank. We had many conversations when I was in grade school, high school and college about how to fairly treat people and a lot of it sunk in.

I was chief financial officer for eleven months and then became President and CEO for the company. My boss returned to his bacteria company. When he told me I was going to be president, he also told me he knew when he hired me that at some point I would become the president. He also told me I was the best chief financial officer he had ever encountered. Being president of a company was one of my goals since high school. In college, I majored in accounting, but I never wanted to be a CPA or a chief financial officer. My dad had suggested I major in accounting because he felt it was a great way to learn about a company from the bottom to the top, and it was a great pathway to the president's office. I absolutely loved the people I worked with at this company, although I must say I had a much harder time with the members of the ownership family. The company and its employees meant only one thing to them, and that was money. "Keep the money flowing, so I don't have to work."

The title of this book included the phrase "Changing Water Into Wine". You might assume that meant good changes for the company and that would be true. However, the change of the water into wine was also referring to the change in me. I believe this turnaround changed my life for the better. Money isn't everything, but being a good husband and a good father is at the top of my list. I became more understanding and patient with those around me. I find it easier to tell others how much they mean to me, and I can now easily recognize how many good things are in my life. I am not wealthy in terms of money, although we are comfortable in our lives. I am actually pleased about that. My greatest accomplishment in life is my kids. They are all honest and hardworking. Would that have been the case if they had lived a life of real privilege? I know for certain that my kids appreciate what they have, because they worked for it and earned it.

My final point, is that the operations of the company were transformed for the good. The employees of the company were transformed in that process, too, and hopefully they learned what it was like to work for someone who genuinely cared about them. Then, there was me. I learned that genuine compassion for your employees pays big dividends.